KT-560-025

Starting with...

Role play

All creatures great and small

Diana Bentley
Maggie Hutchings
Dee Reid

HOPSCOTCH
EDUCATIONAL PUBLISHING

Diana Bentley is an educational consultant for primary literacy and has written extensively for both teachers and children. She worked for many years in the Centre for the Teaching of Reading at Reading University and then became a Senior Lecturer in Primary English at Oxford Brookes University. Throughout her professional life she has continued to work in schools and teach children aged from 5 to 11 years.

Maggie Hutchings has considerable experience teaching KS1 and Early Years. She is a Leading Teacher for literacy in The Foundation Stage and is a Foundation Stage and Art coordinator. Maggie is passionate about the importance of learning through play and that learning should be an exciting and fun experience for young children. Her school's art work has been exhibited in The National Gallery, London.

Dee Reid is a former teacher who has been an independent consultant in primary literacy for over 20 years in many local authorities. She is consultant to 'Catch Up' – a special needs literacy intervention programme used in over 4,000 schools in the UK. She is Series Consultant to 'Storyworlds' (Heinemann) and her recent publications include 'Think About It' (Nelson Thornes) and Literacy World (Heinemann).

212 254

Other titles in the series:

Colour and light
Under the ground
Emergency 999
Into space
At the shops
Fairytales
At the garage/At the airport
At the hospital
On the farm
Water
Ourselves

Other Foundation titles:

Starting with stories and poems:

Self esteem
Self care
A sense of community
Making relationships
Behaviour and self control

A collection of stories and poems

Starting with our bodies and movement

Starting with sounds and letters

The authors would like to thank Jane Whitwell for all her hard work in compiling the resources and poems for the series.

Published by
Hopscotch Educational Publishing Ltd, Unit 2, The Old Brushworks, 56 Pickwick Road, Corsham, Wiltshire, SN13 9BX Tel: 01249 701701

© 2006 Hopscotch Educational Publishing

Written by Diana Bentley, Maggie Hutchings and Dee Reid
Series design by Blade Communications
Cover illustration by Sami Sweeten
Illustrated by Kirsty Wilson
Printed by Colorman (Ireland) Ltd

ISBN 1 905390 19 X

Diana Bentley, Maggie Hutchings and Dee Reid hereby assert their moral right to be identified as the authors of this work in accordance with the Copyright, Designs and Patents Act, 1988.

The authors and publisher would like to thank Chapter One (a specialist children's bookshop) in Wokingham for all their help and support. Email: chapteronebookshop@yahoo.co.uk

All rights reserved. This book is sold subject to the condition that it shall not, by way of trade or otherwise, be lent, hired out or otherwise circulated without the publisher's prior consent in any form of binding or cover other than that in which it is published and without a similar condition, including this condition, being imposed upon the subsequent purchaser.

No part of this publication may be reproduced, stored in a retrieval system, or transmitted, in any form or by any means, electronic, mechanical, photocopying, recording or otherwise, without the prior permission of the publisher, except where photocopying for educational purposes within the school or other educational establishment that has purchased this book is expressly permitted in the text.

Contents

NORWICH CITY COLLEGE LIBRARY
Stock No 212254
Class 372.6 BEN
Cat Proc 05

Acknowledgements

The authors and publisher gratefully acknowledge permission to reproduce copyright material in this book.

'Dinosauristory' by Judith Nicholls. © Judith Nicholls. Reproduced by kind permission of the author.
'Hocus, pocus, diplodocus' by Tom Stanier. © Tom Stanier. Reproduced by kind permission of the author.
'Boa song' by Peggy Drake. © Peggy Drake. Reproduced by kind permission of the author.
'Butterfly inside' by Coral Rumble from *Sugar Cake*, edited by Brian Moses, published by Ginn (1999) © Coral Rumble.
'Zoo Dream' by C John Foster (1994) from *Number Poems*, Oxford University Press. Reproduced by kind permission of the author.

Every effort has been made to trace the owners of copyright of material in this book and the publisher apologises for any inadvertent omissions. Any persons claiming copyright for any material should contact the publisher who will be happy to pay the permission fees agreed between them and who will amend the information in this book on any subsequent reprint.

Introduction

There are 12 books in the series ***Starting with role play*** offering a complete curriculum for the Early Years.

Ourselves	*At the garage/At the airport*
Into space	*Emergency 999*
At the shops	*All creatures great and small*
Colour and light	*Under the ground*
At the hospital	*Fairytales*
On the farm	*Water*

While each topic is presented as a six-week unit of work, it can easily be adapted to run for fewer weeks if necessary. The themes have been carefully selected to appeal to boys and girls and to a range of cultural groups.

Each unit addresses all six areas of learning outlined in the *Curriculum Guidance for the Foundation Stage* and the specific Early Learning Goal is identified for each activity and indicated by this symbol.

Generally, differentiation is achieved by outcome, although for some of the Communication, Language and Literacy strands and Mathematical Development strands, extension activities are suggested for older or more confident learners.

Suggested teaching sequence for each unit

Each week has been organised into a suggested teaching sequence. However, each activity in an area of learning links to other activities and there will be overlap as groups engage with the tasks.

The Core Curriculum: Literacy and Mathematics

Every school will have its own programmes for literacy and mathematics and it is not intended that the activities in the units in this book should replace these. Rather, the activities suggested aim to support any programme, to help to consolidate the learning and to demonstrate how the learning can be used in practical situations.

The importance of role play

'Children try out their most recent learning, skills and competences when they play. They seem to celebrate what they know.'

Tina Bruce (2001) Learning Through Play: Babies, Toddlers and the Foundation Years. London: Hodder & Stoughton.

Early Years practitioners are aware of the importance of play as a vehicle for learning. When this play is carefully structured and managed then the learning opportunities are greatly increased. Adult participation can be the catalyst for children's imaginations and creativity.

Six weeks allows for a role play area to be created, developed and expanded and is the optimum time for inspiring children and holding their interest. It is important not to be too prescriptive in the role play area. Teachers should allow for children's ideas and interests to evolve and allow time for the children to explore and absorb information. Sometimes, the children will take the topic off at a tangent or go into much greater depth than expected or even imagined.

Organising the classroom

The role play area could be created by partitioning off a corner of the classroom with ceiling drapes, an old-style clothes-horse, chairs, boxes, large-scale construction blocks (for example, 'Quadro') or even an open-fronted beach tent/shelter. Alternatively, the whole classroom could be dedicated to the role play theme.

Involving parents and carers

Encourage the children to talk about the topic and what they are learning with their parents or carers at home. With adult help and supervision, they can explore the internet and search for pictures in magazines and books. This enriches the learning taking place in the classroom.

Outside activities

The outdoor classroom should be an extension of the indoor classroom and it should support and enhance the activities offered inside. Boys, in particular, often feel less restricted in outdoor play. They may use language more purposefully and may even engage more willingly in reading and writing activities. In the outdoor area things can be done on a much bigger, bolder and noisier scale and this may connect with boys' preferred learning styles.

Observation in Salford schools and settings noted that boys access books much more readily when there is a book area outdoors.

Resources

Role play areas can be more convincing reconstructions when they are stocked with authentic items. Car boot sales, jumble sales and charity shops are good sources of artefacts. It is a good idea to inform parents and carers of topics well in advance so they can be looking out for objects and materials that will enhance the role play area.

Reading

Every week there should be a range of opportunities for children to participate in reading experiences. These should include:

Shared reading

The practitioner should read aloud to the children from Big Books, modelling the reading process; for example, demonstrating that print is read from left to right. Shared reading also enables the practitioner to draw attention to high frequency words, the spelling patterns of different words and punctuation. Where appropriate, the practitioner should cover words and ask the children to guess which word would make sense in the context. This could also link with phonic work where the children could predict the word based on seeing the initial phoneme. Multiple readings of the same text enable them to become familiar with story language and tune in to the way written language is organised into sentences.

Independent reading

As children become more confident with the written word they should be encouraged to recognise high frequency words. Practitioners should draw attention to these words during shared reading and shared writing. Children should have the opportunity to read these words in context and to play word matching and word recognition games. Encourage the children to use their ability to hear the sounds at various points in words and to use their knowledge of those phonemes to decode simple words.

Writing

Shared writing

Writing opportunities should include teacher demonstration, teacher scribing, copy writing and independent writing. (Suggestions for incorporating shared writing are given each week.)

Emergent writing

The role play area should provide ample opportunities for children to write purposefully, linking their writing with the task in hand. These meaningful writing opportunities help children to understand more about the writing process and to seek to communicate in writing. Children's emergent writing should occur alongside their increasing awareness of the 'correct' form of spellings. In the example below, the child is beginning to have an understanding of letter shapes as well as the need to write from left to right.

Assessment

When children are actively engaged in the role play area this offers ample opportunities for practitioners to undertake observational assessments. By participating in the role play area the practitioner can take time to talk in role to the children about their work and assess their performance. The assessment grid on page 39 enables practitioners to record progress through the appropriate Stepping Stone or Early Learning Goal.

DfES publications

The following publications will be useful:

Progression in Phonics (DfES 0178/2000)
Developing Early Writing (DfES 0055/2001)
Playing with Sounds (DfES 0280/2004)

Planning chart

All creatures great and small

All creatures great and small	Role play area	Personal, Social and Emotional Development	Communication, Language and Literacy	Knowledge and Understanding of the World	Mathematical Development	Creative Development	Physical Development
Week 1	Creating the rainforest	*Be interested, excited and motivated to learn* Discussing pets Talking about dinosaurs	*Extend their vocabulary; explore meaning of new words* Modelling writing Describing a dinosaur Reading poems	*Find out about past and present events* Looking at fossils Making fossils Extending vocabulary	*Use language such as 'greater' and 'smaller'* Looking at scale of dinosaurs Measuring and ordering by size	*Use imagination in art and design* Making a rainforest Making a dinosaur model Creating sound effects	*Show awareness of space* Moving like dinosaurs Creating a dinosaur dance
Week 2	Adding dinosaur skeletons, teeth and eggs Making flying dinosaur mobiles	*Be confident to initiate ideas and speak in familiar group* Thinking about teeth and looking after our teeth	*Attempt writing for different purposes* Making dinosaur riddle books Writing poems	*Find out about features of living things* Talking about dinosaurs coming from eggs Looking at how scientists found out about dinosaurs	*Recognise numerals 1–9* Playing egg game Discussing size Stepping on footprints 1–9	*Explore colour, texture and shape in two or three dimensions* Making headdresses, dinosaur bones, eggs and flying dinosaur mobiles	*Move with control and coordination* Playing dinosaur footprints game and hunting game
Week 3	Creating a desert and polar environment	*Initiate ideas and speak in familiar group* Partner talk Animal protection	*Attempt writing for different purposes* Writing captions and labels Making up new story	*Identify features of living things* Considering large animals and using non-fiction books to gain information	*Count reliably ten objects* Counting in twos Sequencing by size	*Explore colour and texture in two dimensions* Making camouflage marbling Looking at desert and polar regions	*Move with control and coordination* Moving as large animals Playing spiders' web game Playing hide and seek
Week 4	Including birds and other animals in rainforest	*Respond to significant experiences* Talking about respect for animals Sharing feelings about caring for a kitten	*Retell narrative in correct order* Making a class picture story book Making concertina book/ animal alphabet	*Find out about features in natural world* Making a chart of animal features Discussing rainforests	*Use mathematical ideas to solve problems* Making graphs of favourite animals Making and building jigsaws	*Use imagination in art and design* Making animal masks, exotic birds and rainforest flowers	*Move with confidence, imagination and safety* What animal am I? Using Lego to make zoo
Week 5	Adding reptiles Creating their environment	*Work as part of group* Playing 'What animal am I?'	*Extend vocabulary, exploring meaning of new words* Sharing non-fiction books and looking at new vocabulary Making reptile fact book	*Find out about features of living things* Looking at reptiles – snakes, lizards and camouflage	*Use language of 'longer' and 'shorter'* Comparing lengths Making repeating patterns	*Explore colour and texture in two and three dimensions* Making logs and flowers Making snakes/turtle puppets	*Handle tools with control* Cutting skills Moving like snakes
Week 6	Creating scenario for minibeasts	*Show a range of feelings when appropriate* Circle time – care and respect for minibeasts	*Attempt writing for different purposes* Writing labels and invitations	*Find out about features of living things* Creating a wormery Going on a minibeast hunt and exploring pond-life	*Use developing mathematical ideas and methods to solve practical problems.* Counting ladybird spots, Counting in 2s and 10s Looking at symmetry	*Use imagination in art and design* Making minibeast headdress Creating pond, spiders' webs and butterflies Making ugly bug sweets	*Move with control and coordination* Playing spider trap game and frogs in the pond game

In this six-week unit, the children will investigate the animal world. They will concentrate first on the animals that lived on Earth millions of years ago. Then they will move on to explore large creatures which evolved after the dinosaurs – elephants, zebras and birds. Finally, they will consider their favourite animals and round off the unit investigating minibeasts.

In preparation for the unit, collect pictures and posters of dinosaurs. For observing pond-life, sink a shallow container – for example, an upturned dustbin lid or old washing-up bowl – into the ground at the start of the unit. Fill it with water and add some pondweed. Allow the children to observe regularly for wildlife. Hang a nesting box in a safe and secluded area of the garden or playground and provide a bird feeder and/or birdbath. If possible, towards the end of the unit, arrange for the class to visit a local pond, a wildlife park or a conservation zoo. It might also be possible to arrange for a reptile owner to visit the school.

At the end of the unit the class will have made:
- a rainforest, dinosaur masks, dinosaur skeletons, dinosaur eggs, dinosaur teeth
- a desert and a polar environment
- rainforest birds and flowers
- snakes and lizards
- a pond scene, a bird feeder and a wormery.

WEEK 1

The role play area

During this week the children will create a **rainforest**, a large **dinosaur model** and some **fossils**. They will talk about dinosaurs and label an outline of a dinosaur.

Creating the rainforest

Resources

Photocopiable:

Dinosaur templates (page 33)

Fiction books:

Dinosaur Roar by Paul and Henrietta Strickland, Puffin (0 140557 02 4)
Bumpus Jumpus, Dinosaurumpus by Tony Mitton, Orchard (1 841212 94 6)
Ten Terrible Dinosaurs by Paul Strickland, Ragged Bears (1 857142 12 8)

Non-fiction books:

New Star Science Foundation Group Discussion Book, Ginn (0 602398 93 8)
DK Eye Wonder: Dinosaur by Sarah Walker, Dorling Kindersley (1 405304 73 1)
DK Readers: Level 1 Dinosaur's Day, Dorling Kindersley (0 751321 39 7)
DK Readers: Level 2 Dinosaur's Dinners, Dorling Kindersley (0 751357 38 3)

Website:

www.usborne-quicklinks.com

Materials:

- Green fabric and drapes
- Large and small boxes
- Tissue and crepe paper
- Laminated dinosaur cards of different sizes to show scale
- Pictures and posters of dinosaurs (www.glsed.co.uk)
- Small decorator's paintbrushes – for example, 3cm
- Parcel tape
- Animal jigsaws and games

Personal, Social and Emotional Development

Continue to be interested, excited and motivated to learn.

Circle time

- ❑ Ask the children to talk about their favourite animals and pets. Ask: What kinds of animals do they have at home? How big are they? What do they eat? Talk about how we care for our pets and why some animals are not suitable as pets.
- ❑ Show pictures and posters of dinosaurs. Ask them if they would like to have any of these animals for a pet. Tell them that these animals lived millions of years ago, before there were people. Ask them to think of a type of animal that looks like a dinosaur today. Perhaps show them pictures of large reptiles and lizards, such as a bearded dragon or an alligator. Tell them that dinosaurs were types of reptiles – animals with scaly skins like crocodiles and lizards.
- ❑ Tell the children that they are going to create a dinosaur world in the role play area where they will be able to use their imagination and find out about dinosaurs. Ask them to bring in model or toy dinosaurs for a collection.

Knowledge and Understanding of the World

Find out about past and present events.

Extending vocabulary

- ❑ Explain to the children why we don't see dinosaurs today. Using an information book (see Resources) to support your answers, discuss the following: When did dinosaurs live on Earth? What did they eat? Why are there no dinosaurs today? (Nobody really knows why, but this could be explained using the theory that a huge rock or meteorite hit Earth from space causing earthquakes, fires and clouds of dust, or that volcanoes erupted and lava killed the plants so the dinosaurs had no food.)

Fossils

- ❑ How do we know that dinosaurs lived on Earth? Explain that scientists have found fossils (bones that have turned to stone) and put them together like a jigsaw. Explain to the children how fossils occur.

Making fossils

- ❑ Make up a mixture of plaster of Paris, sand and water and pour into shallow trays. Insert sticks to represent bones into the mixture and allow to dry. Hide the trays in the sand tray. Tell the children that they are going to be scientists. Give them brushes and ask them to carefully search for the dinosaur bones. How many can they find?
- ❑ Alternatively, cover objects such as shells or sticks with petroleum jelly, insert them into the plaster mix and remove when dry. What can the children see? Look at the shapes, using a magnifying glass. What patterns can the children see?

Creative Development

Use their imagination in art and design and role play.

Making a rainforest

❑ Show the children a picture of a rainforest – for example, from the *Star Science Group Discussion Book* (see Resources). Using tissue paper, crepe paper, cardboard tubes and other collage materials, create a rainforest environment in the role play area. For example, fill the area with large ferns, trees and vines. Hang branches from the ceiling. Allow the children to design, draw and cut out the materials as independently as possible.

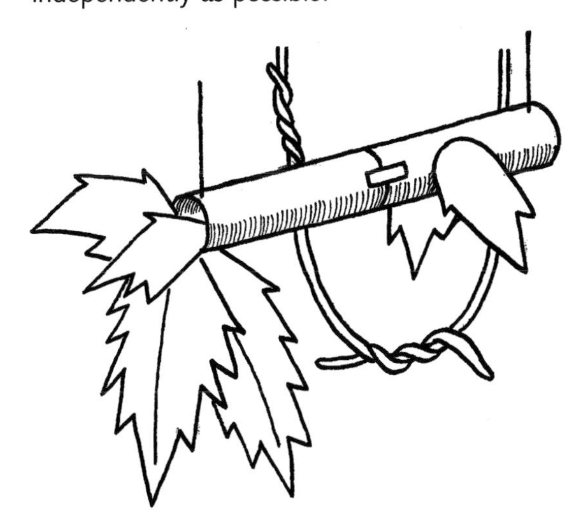

Making a large dinosaur model

❑ Discuss with the children which large model dinosaur you should make. Provide a selection of boxes, including one large box for the body. Place a bag of sand inside the large box for stability. Under the direction of the children, an adult should build the dinosaur, using smaller boxes. These will need to be secured firmly with parcel tape and staples. If necessary, insert a length of dowel through the construction. The tail section could be constructed separately and added later. (NB: this may need to be supported by string from the ceiling.) Use cones of card to create spines along the dinosaur's back. Cover the whole structure with kitchen paper and either watered down PVA glue or cellulose paste. When dry, paint and add scales (see Mathematical Development). Display in or near the role play area.

Dinosaur sound effects

❑ Many websites have dinosaur sound effects (see Resources). Help the children to make a tape of sounds the dinosaurs might have made. (NB: leave gaps of silence and quiet sounds on the tape.) Leave the recording in the role play area to provide authentic background sounds for the children's imaginative play.

Mathematical Development

Use language such as 'greater', 'smaller', 'heavier' and 'lighter'

Mathematical language

❑ Look at pictures and posters of dinosaurs that show the scale of size. Talk to the children about the fact that not all dinosaurs were large – for example, compsognathus was tiny! To give an idea of scale, relate dinosaur size to animals familiar to the children. For example, brachiosaurus was probably the size and weight of 15 elephants. Encourage the children to make comparisons and use early mathematical language, such as 'That dinosaur is huge. It is much bigger than that one,' and 'This is a smaller dinosaur than that one.'

Measuring (outside)

❑ Tell the children that some dinosaurs were so huge they were bigger than the classroom. For example, stegosaurus was about eight metres long. To demonstrate this length, ask one child to hold a ball of wool while another child pulls out the wool. Use a metre stick to mark off eight metres. Do the same for triceratops (11 metres) and diplodocus (28 metres). Inside, staple the lengths of wool to the classroom (going round the corners if necessary).

Ordering by size

❑ Photocopy page 33 and enlarge or reduce the pictures to make a set of cards with dinosaurs of different sizes. Ask the children to order them by size, starting with the smallest or the biggest. Ask them to show you a dinosaur which is smaller/larger than another one.

Three-dimensional shapes

- As the large box model dinosaur is being constructed, talk about the shapes the children are using – for example, cubes, cuboids and cones. Ask the children how many sides/corners this shape has. Challenge them to find another cube shape.

Tessellating shapes

- Prepare a large number of diamond-shaped cards as scales for the model dinosaur (see Creative Development). The colour of card will depend on the colours chosen for the model. On the table, challenge the children to fit the shapes together without any gaps. Talk about the scaly skin covering dinosaurs. Tell the children to reproduce their pattern on the class model of the dinosaur. They should glue their shapes to the model.

Extension

- Give the children a number of triangle-shaped cards. Ask them to fit the shapes together without any gaps. They should then stick their triangle shapes to the dinosaur body.

Communication, Language and Literacy

Extend their vocabulary, exploring the meaning and sounds of new words.

Listening

- Read a dinosaur poem to the class (page 34). Encourage them to join in and learn some of it by heart.
- Read a dinosaur story to the class (see Resources). If possible, use a big book version and point at the text as you read.

Modelled writing

- Draw a large outline of a dinosaur. Ask the children to think of descriptive words related to size – for example, 'huge', 'enormous', 'gigantic', 'massive' and 'immense'. Write these inside the dinosaur outline. Ask the children to help you to make up a sentence for each adjective – for example, 'The huge brontosaurus lifted its long neck. The gigantic tyrannosaurus attacked the stegosaurus.' Talk about the writing process as you write, describing how you use capital letters and full stops.

Writing labels

- Looking at posters or information books, talk to the children about the appearance of the dinosaurs. Ask them to describe their claws or their tails. For example, they may come up with 'sharp claws', 'fierce eyes', 'scaly skin' and so on. Write these descriptions on pieces of card; invite some children to come out, read the labels and decide where to position them on the dinosaur outline.

Extension

- Display a dinosaur poster in the role play area and ask the children to write labels to describe dinosaurs. Remind them to use some of the adjectives discussed earlier. Refer to these labels frequently.

Physical Development

Show awareness of space of themselves and others.

Movement

- Practise moving like the dinosaurs. Make heavy plodding movements like a diplodocus or light, fast running movements like a compsognathus. Lift long necks like reaching up to eat leaves from a tall tree.

Dance

- Make up a dinosaur dance to show variations in movement such as slow and heavy, light and fast, creeping and pouncing. Use percussion instruments or a piece of music to accompany the dance.

WEEK 2

The role play area

During this week the role play area will be developed further and used for imaginative play. The children will add **dinosaur skeletons**, **dinosaur teeth** and **dinosaur eggs** to the role play area. They will make a flying **dinosaur mobile** and each child will make a **dinosaur headdress** to wear.

Resources

Fiction books:

Harry and the Bucket Full of Dinosaurs by Ian Whybrow, Puffin (0 140569 80 4) and other books in the same series
Saturday Night at the Dinosaur Stomp by Carol Diggory Shields, Walker Books (0 744563 45 3)

Non-fiction books:

Gone for Ever Tyrannosaurus Rex, Heinemann (0 431166 00 5) and other dinosaur titles in this series
Usborne Beginners: Dinosaurs by Stephanie Turnball, Usborne (0 746055 85 4)
I am a Tyrannosaurus by Karen Wallace, HodderWayland (0 750242 58 2) and other books in the same series
Mouth and Teeth, 'What do animals have?' series, Heinemann (0 431153 14 0) and other books in the same series

Poetry:

Dinosaur Poems by John Foster, Oxford University Press (0 192763 05 9)

ICT:

'Colour Magic 3', Research Machines.
www.rm.com/primary/products

Video:

Walking with Dinosaurs, BBC Worldwide Publishing (ASIN B0000 4CZTO)

Materials:

- Shoe boxes or similar
- Plastic eggs
- Fillable plastic Easter eggs (available from hobby shops)
- Air-hardening clay
- Pebbles (river pebbles – available from 'pound shops' or garden centres)
- Straws
- Sticks
- Clay tools

Website:

www.enchantedlearning.com

Making dinosaurs

Personal, Social and Emotional Development

Be confident to initiate ideas and speak in a familiar group.

Circle time

- Explain that the children are going to think about their teeth. Why do they think we have teeth? Pass around a plate with small pieces of bread and butter. Tell children to take one piece each and to bite into the bread. Then they should look closely at the marks their teeth have left. Explain that these are our biting teeth, or 'incisors', found at the front of the mouth. Tell them to take a second bite. This time they should concentrate on the chewing action, just before they swallow the bread. Explain that our chewing teeth are called molars.
- Tell the children to look at each other's teeth and to see the differences in shape between incisors and molars. Ask them why they are different shapes.
- Ask the children if they eat meat or just vegetables. Explain about carnivores and herbivores. Tell them that some dinosaurs were carnivores and others were herbivores. Look at pictures to see if it is possible to tell whether the dinosaur was a carnivore or a herbivore. Meat eaters had sharp teeth that faced backwards. Ask: Why do you think that was? Herbivores had flat teeth rather like horses do. Ask: Why do you think that was? Make comparisons with cats, dogs, horses and sheep.

Knowledge and Understanding of the World

Find out about and identify some features of living things.

Dinosaur eggs

- Talk about how dinosaurs were born by adult dinosaurs laying eggs. These eggs were different shapes and sizes. Talk about hatching and relate this to birds hatching out of their eggs.
- Tell the children that scientists can find out what dinosaurs ate by grinding up and testing fossilised droppings! These are called 'coprolites'.
- Talk again about why dinosaurs might have become extinct and explain that some of the animals today evolved from dinosaurs – for example, reptiles, elephants and birds.
- If possible, show some clips from *Walking with Dinosaurs* (see Resources) or another information film about dinosaurs.
- Sort the collection of toy dinosaurs into groups of carnivores and herbivores.

Creative Development

Explore colour, texture, shape in two or three dimensions.

Making headdresses

- Make a headband for each child. Ask children to draw the head or whole body of a dinosaur on card. Decorate and fix to a band at the front. Encourage the children to wear their dinosaur headgear and get into role. Create scenarios for the children to act out.

Dinosaur bones

- Give each child a piece of paper and tell them to use straws to create a dinosaur skeleton. When they are happy with their outline they should glue the straws to the paper. Then they should paint the skeleton with PVA glue and sprinkle with sand.

Mini dinosaur environments in boxes

- Provide shoe boxes, or similar, and a selection of collage materials to create a dinosaur environment – for example, green paper for the grass, blue paper for the sky and reflective paper for a pond. The children may like to make trees from play dough or paper. They should add stones for boulders and, finally, a model dinosaur.

Clay craft – dinosaur eggs

- Make air-hardening clay from 1 cup of cornflour, 2 cups of bicarbonate of soda and 1.25 cups of water. Cook over a medium heat, stirring constantly, until like a thick dough. Turn out onto a board and knead lightly. Cover with a damp cloth until cool. When exposed to air, the clay will dry very hard and can be painted and glazed. (Keep unused clay in silver foil.) Encourage the children to mould and shape dinosaur eggs. They should add texture or patterns, using simple clay tools.

Making a baby dinosaur

- Give each child a plastic fillable Easter egg and some clay. Ask them to make a baby dinosaur to fit inside their egg. Place the dinosaurs in the eggs when dry and use the role play area as a hatching area.

Flying dinosaur mobiles

- Provide a selection of collage materials and card. Tell the children to look at pictures of flying dinosaurs and then draw these on thin card and cut them out. Ask the children to colour them, getting ideas from posters and illustrations. Suspend the flying dinosaurs on a wire coat hanger from the ceiling in the role play area.

Dinosaur teeth

- Mould dinosaur teeth from the clay or salt dough (bake to harden). Hide them in the role play area.

ICT

- Give the children the opportunity to draw a dinosaur using software such as 'Colour Magic' (see Resources).

Mathematical Development

ELG *Recognise numerals 1–9.*

Pebble eggs game

- You will need some pebbles to represent dinosaur eggs, two whiteboards and dry wipe pens. Draw an imaginary dinosaur nest on each board and place them by a pair of children. Child A picks up some pebbles and shows them to Child B, who counts them. Child A turns away and drops one, two or three 'eggs' into a container. He turns back and shows Child B the remaining 'eggs'. Child B says how many 'eggs' were dropped. If correct, he draws an egg in his nest. They take turns. After six goes, the winner is the one with the most eggs in his nest.

Eggs – size

- Prepare a selection of dinosaur egg shapes of different sizes cut out of card. Ask the children to order the eggs according to size.

Eggs – matching

- Mark numbers on the egg cards used for sorting by size. Ask the children to put the correct number of pebble eggs on each card.

Dinosaur footprints (outside)

- Outside, draw large dinosaur footprints in playground chalks. Number the footprints 1 to 10. Direct the children to go to different footprints using different actions – for example, hop to footprint number 8, jump to footprint number 2, and so on.
- Challenge the children to find the right footprint – for example; Can you stand on the footprint one after number 5?, Can you stand on the footprint two less than 3?, and so on.

Extension

- Play the dinosaur teaser game. Draw an outline of a dinosaur and put a four by four grid of small boxes inside. Challenge the children to make each column add up to ten.

Making dinosaurs

Communication, Language and Literacy

Attempt writing for different purposes.

Dinosaur riddle books

- Tell the children they are going to make their own dinosaur riddle books. Fold a sheet of A4 paper in half lengthways, then fold it into four zigzag sections. Open out the zigzags, fold down 2cm from the long fold and glue. Cut each fold up to the glued fold to make the flaps. The child should write a clue on each flap and draw a linked picture on the paper below the flap. The clue should hint at the identity of the dinosaur hidden below the flap – for example, on the flap the child writes 'long neck' and underneath draws a picture of a diplodocus. Tell the children to write a title on the top fold – for example, 'Dinosaur Riddles by Ali'.

Extension

- Model for the children how to write a proper riddle – for example, 'I have a long neck and a long tail. I eat plants' (diplodocus). Ask the children to complete their own riddles and pictures.

Writing poetry

- Brainstorm with the children some suitable descriptions of dinosaurs and then link these together to make simple poems. For example,

  Fierce dinosaurs,

  Munching dinosaurs,

  Hunting dinosaurs,

  Down at the swamp.

  Write these poems for the children on the computer. Illustrate with IT-generated drawings (see Creative Development).

Phonics

- Write the names of some dinosaurs on the board and talk about how the long names are divided into syllables – for example, dip/lo/do/cus; bron/to/sau/rus. Ask the children to clap the syllables as you say the words.

Physical Development

Move with control and coordination.

Dinosaur footprints game

- Using the dinosaur footprints drawn on the playground in Mathematical Development, tell the children to move around the footprints, using the different dinosaur movements explored last week. When you call STOP, also call out a number – for example, 3. Children have to quickly stand in threes on a footprint. (NB: it is possible to use hoops instead of drawn footprints.)

Hunting game

- Ask the children to draw and cut out large dinosaur footprints from sugar paper. Tell them to write a number from 1 to 10 on each footprint. Fix the footprints to the floor or playground with sticky tack. Give each child a beanbag. Tell the children to prowl and stalk as if they are dinosaurs hunting for their prey. Then call out a number. The children stop where they are and look for a footprint with that number. They then try to gently throw their beanbag onto a footprint with that number.

WEEK 3

The role play area

During this week the role play area will remain as a forest but children's play will revolve around large animals in the world today. They will create collages of **desert** and **polar** environments and discover which creatures live in these extreme temperatures. They will make **camouflage pictures** and **paper weave a patchwork elephant**.

Resources

Photocopiables:

Poems and songs 1 and 2 (pages 34 and 35)
Patchwork elephant (page 36)
Sequencing animals (page 37)

Fiction books:

Polar Bear, Polar Bear by Bill Martin Jnr, Puffin (0 140545 19 0)
We're going on a Lion Hunt by David Axtell, Macmillan (0 333741 49 8)
Walking through the Jungle by Julie Lacome, Walker (0 744536 43 X)
Elmer the Elephant by David McKee, Red Fox (0 099697 20 3)
Rumble in the Jungle by Charles Andreae, Franklin Watts (1 860398 26 X)
Giraffes Can't Dance by Charles Andreae, Orchard (1 841215 65 1)

Non-fiction books:

I Know That! Rainforest Animals by Claire Llewellyn, Franklin Watts (0 749651 70 9)
Elephants by Patricia Kendell, 'In the wild' series, Hodder Wayland (0 750240 03 2)
Polar Bear 'Animals in Danger' series, Heinemann (0 431001 36 7)

Poetry:

What Fun to be a Hippo, ed Wendy Cooling, Franklin Watts (0 749638 40 0)

Music and songs:

The Animal Boogie (with CD) by Debbie Harter, Barefoot Books (1 841489 14 X)
Birds and Beasts by Sheena Hodge, A & C Black (0 713656 53 0)
Warm Up and Work Out With the Sticky Kids, PO Box 176, Glasgow, G11 5YJ

Videos:

Amazing Animals: Animal Hunters, DK Vision (0 75136 16 4)
Animal Neighbours, DK Vision (0 751361 70 4)
Giant Animals, DK Vision (0 751361 71 2)

Materials:

- Shallow tray
- Marbling inks
- Pictures, posters and books about animals
- 'Linking Elephants' (available from educational suppliers such as NES)

Animal habitats

Personal, Social and Emotional Development

Initiate ideas and speak in a familiar group.

Partner talk

- Show the children pictures of hedgehogs, cats and birds. Talk about how animals protect themselves in different ways – some hide; some fight. Ask the children to work in pairs to select a creature and discuss in which ways the animal might protect itself – for example, a cat could hiss and scratch. A cheetah could run away very quickly and its colouring makes it difficult to see. Give the children a speaking frame to support their contributions to the group – for example, 'I am looking at a picture of a … (cat). If a … (cat) is frightened it can … (run away very fast) or it can … (scratch another animal with its sharp claws).' Invite the children to talk to the class about ways their animal protects itself.

Animal protection

- Remind the children that dinosaurs became extinct millions of years ago. Talk about how some animals are in danger of becoming extinct today. Why might these animals be in danger? Talk about preserving habitats in this country and abroad. Explain how some zoos have protected these animals and that now many are able to return to the wild.

Knowledge and Understanding of the World

Find out about and identify some features of living things.

Finding information

- Brainstorm with the class animals that are really big – elephant, gorilla, bear, giraffe, rhinoceros, hippopotamus, moose, lion, tiger, kangaroo, zebra, camel and polar bear. Tell the children that they are going to find some information about these animals. Ask the children to work with a partner and to look through some non-fiction books (see Resources). Give each pair a set of questions on cards – for example; Where does the animal live? What does it eat? What colour is its coat? Is it dangerous?
- Ask them to decide which is the most interesting picture in their book and to show this to the class as they talk about what they have discovered.

Camouflage

- Show the children pictures of animals that have used camouflage to protect themselves – zebras, tigers, lizards, snakes and chameleons. Can the children see the animals in the pictures? Talk about why animals use camouflage. Can they think why a zebra has a striped coat? (Grass, movement, shimmering in the African heat.) Why do they think a polar bear has a white coat? Why do they think a camel is a light brown colour?

Creative Development

Explore colour and texture in two dimensions.

Camouflage marbling

- You will need marbling inks, a shallow tray and water. Drop marbling inks into the tray of water and make patterns with a stick or the end of a paintbrush. Lay an A4 sheet of paper on the inky water. Remove and allow to dry. Cut off about a third of each sheet of marbled paper and give it to individual children. Ask them to draw an outline of an animal and then cut it out. Glue the animal onto the rest of the marbled sheet. Ask the children to comment. Can they see the animal clearly? Explain that it is camouflaged because its markings blend in with the background. Display the camouflaged animals under the heading 'Can you see the animals?'

Desert and polar landscapes

- Remind the children about animal camouflage. Talk about some animals that are camouflaged in the desert (for example, camels) and animals that are camouflaged in the polar regions (for example, polar bears). Look through non-fiction books to find examples of these habitats. Tell the children they are going to create these landscapes and then the animals that live there. Create the background for the desert animals by applying orangey-yellow paint for the sand to a large sheet of blue paper. (Mixing a little PVA glue with the paint will give texture to the sand.) For the polar landscape either use white blown vinyl wallpaper or paint the snow and ice using white paint on a large blue sheet of paper. Ask the children to draw, paint and cut out animals – for example, camels, snakes and rats or polar bears, arctic foxes and reindeer. Discuss with the children which habitat these animals live in and then ask them to glue the animals on the appropriate background. Display these in or near the role play area.

Weaving

- Read the story *Elmer the Elephant* to the class (see Resources). Talk about how Elmer was different from all the other elephants and how he was not camouflaged. Give each child a copy of page 36, which is an outline of Elmer. Cut the centre into strips for weaving as marked. Give the children strips of coloured paper to weave in and out of Elmer. Place the Elmer elephants in the role play area to show how Elmer contrasts with his environment.

Drawing, using pastel crayons

- Ask the children to make drawings of their favourite big animal, using pastels. Show them how to smudge their drawings and how to superimpose colours.

Communication, Language and Literacy

Attempt writing for different purposes.

Listening

- Read one of the stories about an animal (see Resources). Discuss with the children the beginning, middle and end of the story. Support them as they retell the story in sequence. For example, What happened at the beginning? What happened next?

Rhyming

- Share with the class one of the poems from page 34. Encourage the children to identify the rhyming words and think of further rhyming words. Write these on a large sheet of paper and display near the classroom door. Encourage the children to read them while lining up and to add any new words they find.

Demonstration writing

- Demonstrate to the children how to use an information book to find some interesting facts about animals. Choose an animal and draw a simple outline of it. Then write a caption under your drawing (for example, 'This hippo can walk along the river-bed'), talking about the writing process as you write.

Labels

- Ask the children to write labels for the animals in the desert and polar regions (see Creative Development).

Extension

- Tell the group that they are going to help you to make up a new story about a big animal. (This could be another story about Elmer.) Give them suggestions as to how their story might start. For example, 'A long time ago in a…', 'Once there was a very happy…' or 'George was a very unusual…' Ask them what might happen next. Take one of their suggestions and add it to the story. Continue to develop the story orally and offer suggestions for how it might end. For example, 'So he never went there again,' or 'From that day to this all ... like to eat standing up.' Go over the story, ensuring the group know the sequence and then ask the children to choose different sections of the story and to illustrate their section and write that part of the story. Collect the sections of the story and paste them into a blank scrapbook. Display their story in the role play area.

Mathematical Development

Count reliably up to ten everyday objects.

Counting

- ❑ Look at pictures of different animals. Count legs, horns, ears and so on. Ask: Can you find an animal that has two horns? Can you find an animal that has just one horn? How many twos can you see? (Two horns, two eyes, two front legs, two back legs.)
- ❑ Sing 'Alice the camel had five humps' (page 35) (counting backwards).
- ❑ Sing 'Five little monkeys' (page 34).

Extension

- ❑ Help the children to practise counting to ten in twos. Link this to the pictures of the animals – for example, two eyes, two ears and so on.

Sorting

- ❑ Provide pictures from magazines, old books and posters. Ask the children to cut them out. Use these pictures to sort the animals by, for example, long tail/short tail/no tail; horns/no horns; wild/domestic; all one colour/stripes or spots.

Sequencing

- ❑ Either use a commercially produced resource for sequencing creatures of different sizes (for example, Linking Elephants – see Resources) or photocopy page 37 onto thin card; colour, cut out and laminate it. Ask the children to put the animals into size order and to use the language of comparison. For example, 'This is the biggest lion.' or 'This lion is smaller than that lion.'

Physical Development

Move with control and coordination.

Fine motor skills

- ❑ See weaving and cutting in Creative Development.

Movement

- ❑ Ask the children to pretend to be a big animal and to walk on all fours. Tell them to vary the speed of their walking. Invite them to keep one leg off the floor as they move. Ask: Is this more difficult?

Music and movement

- ❑ Arrange the children in a circle, holding hands in an arch to represent the edges of a spider's web. Ask one child to be the elephant and to weave in and out of the arches. While the child moves, the rest of the class chant:

  'An elephant began to play, Upon a spider's web one day. He thought it such tremendous fun. He called for another elephant to come.'

  Then choose another child to hold hands with the first 'elephant' and off they go weaving in and out of the circle while the others chant the rhyme.
- ❑ Listen to the recording of 'Walking through the jungle' from *Warm Up and Work Out with the Sticky Kids* (see Resources) or some other suitable music – for example, from *The Jungle Book* or *Lion King*. Tell the children to move around the room, mimicking the movement of the animals.

Outside

- ❑ Play hide-and-seek in the garden or playground. The children might like to use dressing-up clothes for camouflage.

WEEK 4

The role play area

During this week the children will look at other animals, familiar and less familiar to them. The role play area will be further developed to include birds and other animals. Children will make **animal masks, exotic birds with their nests**, and **flowers** for the rainforest.

Resources

Photocopiables:

Poems and Songs 2 (page 35)

Fiction books:

Animal Stories For the Very Young by Sally Grindley (ed.), Kingfisher Books (0 753407 30 2)
Slow Loris by Alexis Deacon, Red Fox (0 099414 26 0)

Non-fiction books:

Toucans: Animals of the Rainforest, Raintree (1 844210 92 8)
Howler Monkeys: Animals of the Rainforest by Sandra Donovan, Raintree (0 739868 36 5)
Journey to the Rainforest by Tim Knight, Oxford University Press (0 199107 31 9)
Rainforest Animals: Me and My World by Vic Parker, Franklin Watts (0 749656 50 6)

Music and songs:

Big Steps, Little Steps (CD and songbook) by Mary Maunder, Kindescope, www.kindescope.com
Bobby Shaftoe, Clap Your Hands by Sue Nicholls, A & C Black (0 713635 56 8)
Bingo Lingo by Helen MacGregor, A&C Black (0 731650 75 3)

Websites:

www.nationalgeographic.com
www.kinderstart.com (graded jigsaws; pieces slot into appropriate shapes)
www.enchantedlearning.com

Materials:

- Tissue paper
- Paper plates
- Coloured feathers
- Binoculars
- Pine cones
- Dowel
- Coloured pipe cleaners
- Icing sugar
- Small sweets (dolly-mixtures)

Birds and other animals

Personal, Social and Emotional Development

Respond to significant experiences, showing a range of feelings when appropriate.

Circle time

- Talk about how it is very important that people respect all animals. Ask the children if anyone is frightened of an animal. What makes them frightened? Ask the group what they think the child should do if an animal they do not like comes near them. Talk about teasing and how unhappy that can make people. Link this to teasing and taunting animals.
- Ask the children to help you to make a list of ways to treat wild animals. For example, give the animals plenty of space to move away from you, keep very quiet and still, do not run away and do not poke them with a stick.

Drama

- Tell the children to imagine that they have a little kitten on their lap. Tell them to stroke it gently, making sure they stroke the fur the right way. Ask: Is your kitten purring to show it is happy? How do you feel? Explain that you are going to make a loud noise and their kittens will jump off their laps and scratch them with their back claws. Clap your hands and then ask the children how they felt when the kitten hurt them. Ask: Are you cross with the kitten? What will you do next? How will you tempt the kitten to sit on your lap again?

Mathematical Development

Use developing mathematical ideas and methods to solve practical problems.

Graphs

- Divide a large sheet of paper into columns and label each column with a wild animal of the children's choice. Give each child a square of sticky paper and ask them to write their name on it. Ask the children to think of their favourite wild animal and to come out and stick their square in the right column. Interpret the data together – for example, the most popular animal is... and Only one child likes ... best.

Jigsaws

- Cut out pictures of wild animals and laminate them. Cut the pictures into jigsaws of two to five pieces.

Extensions

- Access the jigsaw site and ask the children to complete the jigsaws (see Resources) according to ability and experience.
- Show the children a picture (from a non-fiction book) of little chicks. Tell the children that the farmer wants to buy six chicks from the market. He has some basket but each basket can only fit three chicks. How many baskets will he need? Encourage the children to experiment with counters to represent the chicks and small boxes to represent the baskets. Experiment further with varying numbers of chicks.

Counting

- Share the counting poem 'Zoo dream' on page 35.

Communication, Language and Literacy

Retell narrative in the correct sequence, drawing on language patterns of stories.

Listening

- Read an animal story to the class (see Resources). Discuss the story with the children and encourage them to join in when you read it again.

Making a picture story

- Retell the story of 'The Little Red Hen' to the class. You will need four sheets of A4 paper and 12 speech bubbles for the children to write in. Act out the story with different groups of children taking the parts of the little red hen, the goat, the cat and the rat.

Then, using four A4 sheets of paper, make a picture story. On the first sheet draw the little red hen by a field of corn and a speech bubble, 'Who will help me cut the corn?' On the second sheet draw the little red hen with some stalks of corn and a windmill in the background and the same speech bubble as above. On the third sheet draw the little red hen with a bag of flour and on the fourth sheet draw the little red hen with a loaf of bread. Retell the story and when you come to the animal responses demonstrate how to write 'Not I.' Then ask three children to complete their speech bubbles and stick them next to the A4 sheet, using sticky tack. Continue with the story and invite a further three children to complete their speech bubbles and stick them on. Do the same until the fourth sheet when you should demonstrate writing 'I will.' Then ask the final three children to complete their speech bubbles. Retell the story again, pointing to the speech bubbles and asking the children to join in.

Making a zigzag book

- Encourage the children to browse through non-fiction books and encyclopedias. Ask them to find pictures and information about their favourite animals. Show them how to make a simple zigzag book. Ask them to draw pictures of wild animals found in this country (such as a fox, rabbit, mouse, bird, fish, deer, badger or squirrel) on each page and label or add captions according to ability. Leave the zigzag books in the role play area for the children to explore.

Making an animal alphabet

- Write out the alphabet, distributed over three columns, on an A3 sheet. Sing the alphabet with the children (to the tune of 'Auld lang syne') and ask them to suggest animals for each letter. Invite a child to draw the correct animal next to the letter. Help all the children to associate the phoneme with the animal name. Display the animal alphabet near the role play area and encourage the children to link the animal with its initial phoneme – for example, 'd' for dog.

Music and songs

- Sing songs from *Bingo Lingo* (see Resources), such as 'Old MacGregor had a zoo', 'The hungry rabbit' or 'The bat and cat'.

Knowledge and Understanding of the World

Observe, find out about and identify features in the natural world.

Animal features

- Make a simple chart on the board and write the following features – fur, feathers, scales, coat and skin. Write the names of some animals on the board and, if possible, look at pictures in non-fiction books. Ask the children which category the animal should go in – for example, does it have a fur coat, feathers and so on? In the role play area encourage the children to challenge one another with riddles – for example, 'I have a thick furry coat and a waggly tail and I bark. What am I?'
- Bring in examples of different fabrics that are similar to animal coats – for example, furry fabrics and feathers. Leave in a box in the role play area for children to handle.

The rainforest

- Talk about rainforests. Explain that they are hot, humid and steamy. Look at a non-fiction book showing some of the fauna of the rainforest – for example, toucan, spider monkey, macaw, boa constrictor, poison-arrow frog and sloth. Some animals live on the forest floor while others live in the canopy of trees. Using a search engine, enter 'rainforest sounds' and let children click on various pictures and hear the sounds of the creatures living there. Take the children on an imaginary expedition to explore the rainforest. Wear hats to protect yourselves from the sun. Give a Sir David Attenborough style commentary about the creatures you can see on the forest floor and in the trees above. Encourage the children to use the binoculars to get a better view of the shy creatures.

Creative Development

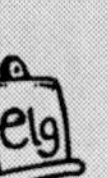

Use their imagination in art and design.

Animal masks

- Cut paper plates in half. Cut out a shape for the nose. Cut holes for the eyes. Provide a selection of paints and collage materials. Ask the children to create an animal mask of their choice. Pierce holes on either side of the plate and add fine elastic. Encourage children to wear their mask when entering the role play area and to move in a way appropriate to the animal they represent. Provide hooks for the masks so that the children can use them freely in their play.

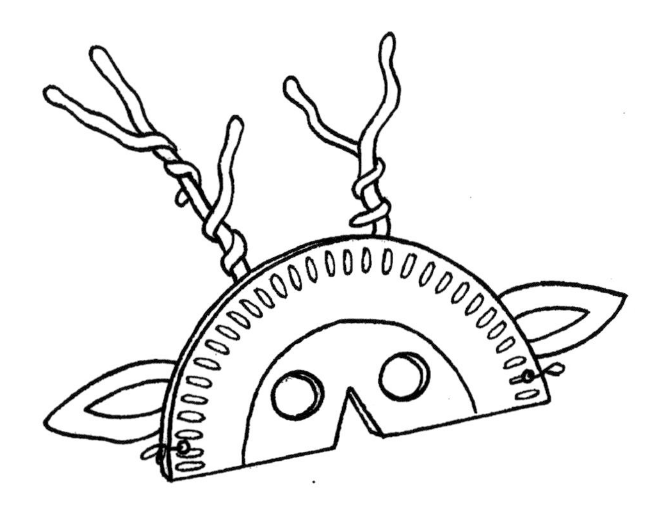

Exotic birds

- Look at pictures of tropical birds in books or on websites. Listen to the birdsong and try to replicate some of the calls. Provide a selection of collage materials and brightly coloured feathers. Ask the children to draw and cut out bird shapes. Encourage them to decorate their birds with the materials and feathers and to be as innovative as they like! Ask the children to give their birdcalls as they stick their birds onto large sheets of green paper to represent the treetops. Talk through a scenario in which it is night-time and all the birds are sleeping. Then at the first light of dawn the birds begin to awake and start their calls, quietly at first and then more loudly.

Create flowers for the rainforest

- You will need tissue and crepe paper, pine cones, garden sticks or thin dowelling and coloured pipe cleaners. Show the children some ideas from the web. Allow the children to experiment and try making their own flowers to place in the role play area.

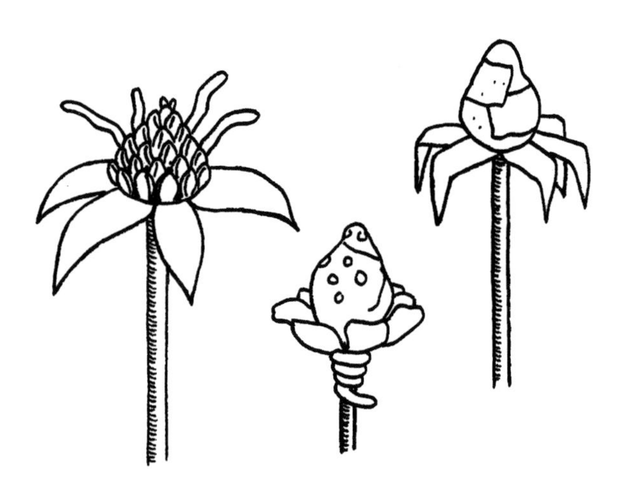

Observational drawings

- Share with the children a range of non-fiction books showing wild animals or creatures of the rainforest. Demonstrate how to look closely at a picture of an animal and then draw the animal based on the observation. Create a 'washing line' to display the finished pictures across the role play area.

Music and songs

- Sing 'A hedgehog is very prickly' from *Bobby Shaftoe, Clap Your Hands* (see Resources).
- Sing and play 'Mrs Bear' from *Bobby Shaftoe, Clap Your Hands* (see Resources).

Bird's-nest treats

- Give each child a plain biscuit to decorate. Use a stiff mixture of icing sugar and water to stick coloured 'eggs' into the 'nest'. The eggs can be any small sweets, such as dolly mixtures. Tell the children to put three eggs in their nest.

Physical Development

Move with confidence, imagination and safety.

Moving like an animal

- Tell the children to think of the rainforest animals they have been learning about. Tell them that they are spiders living on the forest floor. First they should keep very still, then they see some food and then they should dart out on their eight legs to capture it. Then they should lie on their backs and wave their arms and legs in the air to represent the spider tying up its prey. Then they should become boa constrictors, slithering along a branch looking for their next meal. Next they should be howler monkeys, sitting on their haunches on a bough in the tree. Then a loud noise disturbs them and they call out as they swing from branch to branch. Finally, they should be sloths, lying on their backs and using both arms and legs to hang onto a branch above. Challenge them to move so slowly that you can't see them do it.

Which animal am I?

- Invite the children to move like one of the rainforest animals. Ask the others to guess which animal they are.

Music and movement

- Move around like Connie the cow in *Big Steps, Little Steps* (see Resources).

Fine motor movement

- Using either a commercially made zoo or a Lego construction, challenge children in the role play area to manipulate zoo animals in and through, over and under the buildings. Challenge them to use the correct language to describe the movements the animals are making.

Tracing

- Give the children animal templates. Ask them to hold the template firmly with one hand and use their writing hand to trace round the perimeter. Give six children a different template each and challenge them to create a picture, with one traced picture of each animal on a sheet of A3 paper. Display the finished sheets in the role play area.

WEEK 5

The role play area

During this week the children will investigate reptiles. They will learn about these cold-blooded creatures and make a suitable environment where lizards might live. They then make **lizards** and **snakes** in a variety of mediums and place them in the role play area. They will make a **turtle puppet** and write a **reptile fact book**. They will experiment with movement and sound, taking on the role of scientists, investigating reptiles in the forest and other environments.

Resources

Photocopiable:

Poems and songs 2 (page 35)

Fiction books:

The Mixed Up Chameleon by Eric Carle, Puffin (0 140506 42 X)
The Selfish Crocodile by Faustin Charles, Bloomsbury (0 747541 93 0)
Hissing Hattie by Melanie Joyce, 'The Ladybird Animal Stories', Ladybird (1 844220 43 5) and others in the same series

Non-fiction books:

Boa Constrictors: Animals of the Rainforest by Christopher Butz, Raintree (1 844210 90 1)
Imagine… You are a Crocodile by Karen Wallace, HodderWayland (0 750243 18 X)
Reptiles, 'What's the Difference?' series, HodderWayland (0 750241 51 9)
Reptiles, 'Animal Young' series, Heinemann (0 431030 74 X)
Snakes, 'Really Wild' series Heinemann (0 431028 73 7)
Snake by Barrie Watts, 'Watch It Grow' series, Franklin Watts (0 74944 32 X)

Materials:

- Pipe cleaners
- Cardboard tubes
- Tissue paper
- Crepe paper

Website:

www.nationalgeographic.com

Personal, Social and Emotional Development

Work as part of a group.

What animal am I?

- Sit the class facing a chair. One child goes out of the room. (An adult should accompany younger children.) The rest of the group thinks of an animal for the child to be. The child returns to sit on the chair and can ask five questions to find out which animal he or she is. This takes practice so, when first playing this game, help the children to think of good questions. For example, How many legs have I got? Do I have fur, scales or skin? Is my coat plain or patterned? Do I live in the wild or with people? To further simplify the game, limit the choice of animal to one in a set of pictures to which the children can refer.

Knowledge and Understanding of the World

Find out and identify some features of living things.

Observing reptiles

- If possible, arrange for an expert to bring reptiles into school for the children to observe.
- Talk about the features of reptiles (bodies covered with scales or horny plates; cold-blooded and rely on the sun to keep them warm; shed their skin as they grow; most lay eggs).
- Look through information books and show pictures of different reptiles – lizards, snakes, crocodiles, alligators, turtles and tortoises. Ask the children if they can see any similarities between these animals. Point out that snakes and tortoises have similar shaped heads. Look at their skin. Explain that it is dry and scaly. Ensure that the children understand that snakes are not slimy to touch. Talk about how some reptiles have a hard shell. Discuss why this might be (protection).

Snakes

- Look at information books and websites about snakes. Ask the children where snakes' ears are. Explain that snakes do not have external ears but they do have inner ears. They can hear movement from ground vibrations. Explain that a snake uses its forked tongue to smell things. Talk about the different types of snakes. Some are constrictors (they crush their prey) while others are poisonous (they inject venom into their prey).

Camouflage

- Revisit the work done on camouflage earlier in the unit. Tell the children to look at the patterns or markings on the skin of reptiles. Ask the children why they think reptiles have these markings.

Reptile facts

- Start a reptiles 'fact file'. Encourage the children to ask questions and to investigate in books. Can they find out: Where do some reptiles live? Where do they lay their eggs? How do reptiles move? What do reptiles eat? How do they catch their prey? Discuss answers to these questions. List the questions in a 'fact file' and display it in the role play area. Encourage children to recall the answers.

Mathematical Development

Use language such as 'longer' and 'shorter' to compare lengths.

Comparison of lengths

- Tell the children to roll different lengths of play dough and to arrange the 'snakes' in a row. Ask them to identify the longest 'snake', the shortest 'snake' and so on.

Repeating patterns

- Cut out diamonds and triangles from sticky-backed paper. Ask the children to stick the shapes in a pattern along the length of some snake outlines.
- Draw some simple snake outlines and mark the top with a diamond pattern. Start a pattern of colours –

for example, red, brown, black, red, brown, black – and ask the children to continue the pattern along the length of the snake.

Creative Development

Explore colour, texture, shape, form and space in two or three dimensions.

Making logs and flowers

- Tell the children that they are going to make an environment for reptiles. Show them how to make flowers by covering cardboard tubes with shades of brown tissue paper, sometimes scrunching it to give texture. Cut leaf shapes out of green tissue and crepe paper. Scatter these around the logs. Make flowers out of coloured tissue and crepe paper. Place these around the logs in the role play area.

Making snakes

- Snakes can be made from a variety of materials:
  - by folding strips of paper at right angles to form a concertina. Add a head and taper the tail end;
  - by cutting paper in a snake shape and decorating it with crayons;
  - by moulding a dough made from bicarbonate of soda (see Week 2, Creative Development, page 13). Leave to dry and then paint with snake markings;
  - by twisting coloured pipe cleaners or by using a simple sock puppet;
  - by a variation on the sock puppet, which is to use a straightened wire coat hanger (with any sharp ends folded in with pliers) inserted into an old tie. Add stuffing and glue down the ends (thin end for the tail and thicker end for the head). Add eyes from black or green felt;
  - by rubbing green, brown and red crayon on long strips of paper with a bicycle tyre underneath, then cutting out snake shapes. The texture of the tyre creates a very effective snakeskin;
  - by drawing spirals on paper, cutting round the lines to make spiral snakes and colouring them with diamond patterns. Dangle the snakes from cotton thread on a 'washing line' in the role play area to watch the snakes curl and uncurl.
- Discuss with the children where they want their snake to be displayed. Talk again about camouflage – for example, if they want their snake to be positioned in the desert environment then they should think which colours will blend into the sand background.

Making lizards

- Lizards can be made by drawing a simple outline on card and cutting it out, or by moulding a bicarbonate of soda dough and then painting it. Allow the children the opportunity to look at pictures of lizards to help their modelling. Talk about the diamond patterning explored in Mathematical Development. Display the snakes and lizards in the role play area, in or around the logs and flowers.

Making reptile skins

- Crumple newspaper into a tight ball. Then open it out to lie flat. The paper will be crinkly. Using sponges, paint the paper shades of green and brown.

Making a turtle puppet

- Use two paper plates for the shell and a green sock for the body, head and tail. Glue or staple the plates together with the sock between them. The legs can be made from sections of cardboard tubes.

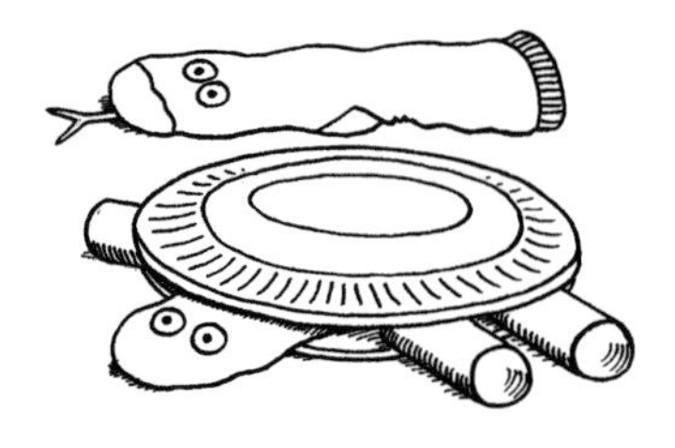

Junk models

- Provide a range of 'junk' materials, especially narrow tubes, and encourage the children to make snakes and other reptiles.

Becoming scientists

- Model and encourage imaginative play in the role play area. Tell the children to imagine they are scientists, investigating reptiles. Ask: Where are they hiding? Are they camouflaged? How many can you find?

Communication, Language and Literacy

Extend their vocabulary, exploring the meanings and sounds of new words.

Listening

- Read 'Crocodile tears' from *Animal Stories for the Very Young* (see Resources – Week 4) or another suitable animal story.
- Read the poem 'Boa song' on page 35.

Animal names

- Use a set of alphabet letters and give each child a letter (exclude q, x, y and z). Write the name of an animal on the board (for example, lion, bear, tiger or snake) and challenge the children to work cooperatively to find the letters needed to spell the name. They should only come out to the front when all the letters are in the right place.

Vocabulary extension

- Share with the children some information books about reptiles or explore websites (see Resources). Engage in play with the children and the models of reptiles they have made. Introduce new vocabulary as you play, such as 'Your lizard's skin feels quite rough; it is scaly,', 'Can you make your snake go slithering through the undergrowth?' and 'Is your lizard sitting very still, waiting to catch its prey?'

Writing labels

- Look again at pictures of reptiles and ensure the children can identify each one – for example, different snakes such as a boa constrictor and python and different lizards such as a monitor and a gecko. Demonstrate writing labels for each of the models the children made in Creative Development. Encourage the children to make their own labels and to place these next to their models.

Extension: Making a reptile fact book

- Give each child in the group a book about A4 size with approximately six pages. Encourage them to look for pictures of reptiles to stick in their books or to draw pictures of reptiles. Demonstrate how to label some features of each reptile – for example, scaly skin, forked tongue or hard shell. Help them to devise captions for their pictures. Discuss with the children what they should write and shape their suggestions into sentences – for example, 'This is a tortoise – it moves very slowly.' or 'This snake squashes its prey.'

Physical Development

Handle tools safely and with increasing control.

Movement

- Tell the children to pretend to be snakes. They should lie on the floor asleep. Early in the morning the temperature is cool so the snakes keep quite still. Then the temperature rises and the snakes begin to slither around, using their flickering tongues to detect prey. At midday the sun is very hot and the snakes curl up in a shady place. Early in the evening, when it is cooler, they move around again, looking for more prey. Allow the children to use hissing sounds to accompany their movements.

Cutting skills

- See Creative Development.

  NB: at the end of this week, write a note to parents telling them that next week there will be an Ugly Bug Ball and the children will be able to dress up as bugs!

WEEK 6

The role play area

This week the children will investigate minibeasts. The children will enter the role play area in the role of minibeasts, create scenarios and investigate their surroundings. They will observe worms in a wormery and watch sea monkeys grow. They will make **minibeast headdresses** and **pond creatures**. At the end of the week, the children will have an Ugly Bug Ball, will **dress up as bugs** and have a party.

Resources

Photocopiables:

Poems and songs 2 (page 35)
The life cycle of the ladybird (page 38)

Fiction books:

The Very Hungry Caterpillar by Eric Carle, Puffin (0 140569 32 4)
The Crunching, Munching Caterpillar by Sheridan Cain, Little Tiger Press (1 854306 41 3)
Centipede's 100 Shoes by Tony Ross, Andersen Press (1 842702 84 X)
The Bugliest Bug by Carol Diggory Shields, Walker (0 744598 13 3)

Non-fiction books:

Butterfly, 'Watch Me Grow' series, Dorling Kindersley (1 405302 42 9)
Frog, 'Watch Me Grow' series, Dorling Kindersley (1 405301 61 9)
Bugs, Bugs, Bugs (Big Book), Dorling Kindersley (0 751361 95 X)
Ladybird, 'Little Nippers' series, Heinemann (0 431163 02 2) and other titles in the series
Walkabouts: Minibeasts by Henry Pluckrose, Franklin Watts (0 749652 64 0)
Insects (Big Book), Heinemann (0 431030 84 7)

Video:

Mini Beasts, DK Vision

Music and songs:

Bobby Shaftoe, Clap Your Hands by Sue Nicholls, A&C Black, (0 713635 56 8)
Michael Finnigin, Tap your Chinnigin by Sue Nicholls, A&C Black, (0 713647 16 7)
Tom Thumb's Musical Maths by Helen MacGregor, A&C Black, (0 713649 71 2)

Materials:

- Paper plates for frogs
- Bugs (toys or from educational suppliers) and viewers (magnifying instruments)

Websites:

www.allthelyrics.com
www.insectlore.com
www.peteyandpetunia.com/UglyBug/UglyBug/htm (the Burl Ives song)

Wildlife:

If you wish to observe live creatures, then crickets, bugs and sea monkeys are available from pet centres selling exotic pets. Many will allow schools to return the creatures at the end of the week. Caterpillars can be ordered from Insect Lore (see above).

Personal, Social and Emotional Development

Respond to significant experiences, showing a range of feelings when appropriate.

Circle time

- Emphasise the need for care and respect for minibeasts when searching for them. Explain that these creatures are tiny and they can easily be damaged. We should not harm them by touching and should always return them to where they were found. It is kinder to look, not touch.
- Read the story of Noah's Ark from the Bible. Discuss how Noah cared for all the animals and saved them from the flood.
- Allow the children to share anxieties about seeing some minibeasts close up. Some may fear that the creatures bite. Talk about the importance of protecting all living creatures.

Knowledge and Understanding of the World

Find out and identify some features of living things.

Creating a wormery

- Take a large, clear container and fill it with soil and thin layers of sand. (An old fish tank is suitable but it is best to divide the space in half lengthways as otherwise any worm activity might happen too much in the centre of the tank and the children won't see much.) Keep the soil damp but not wet. Make very small air holes in the lid. Introduce three or four worms and place a few leaves and small pieces of fruit or vegetable on top of the soil. Spend time with small groups of children observing the actions of the worms and encourage the children to talk about what they observe – for example, wormcasts that might appear on the surface. Add some extra water to the soil and tell the children to see what happens.

Minibeast hunt

- Outside, in a corner of the play area, place a log and an old piece of carpet or a rock, and instruct the children not to touch it. After a few days lift carefully and observe the wildlife that has collected there. Help the children to identify each insect they see.

Mini pond

- Spend time with groups of children observing the mini pond outside. Ask them to tell you about their findings.
- Take out a small amount of the water to observe. Has it changed colour? Is there any wildlife in it? If possible, look at the water under a digital microscope.

Life cycles

- Talk about the life cycle of the ladybird. Using the information on page 38, draw the life cycle of the ladybird and talk to the children about each stage in this process.
- Talk about the life cycle of the frog. Record this on a box (see Communication, Language and Literacy).
- Talk about the life cycle of the butterfly. If desired, order caterpillars (see Resources) and observe their changes through the life cycle.
- Browse through information books to find out more about slugs and snails – their life cycle and hibernation.

Insect body parts

- Look at an outline drawing of an ant. Copy this onto a whiteboard and tell the children the names of the external body parts – head, thorax and abdomen – as you label them. Ask the children which body part the legs come from and which body part the feelers come from.

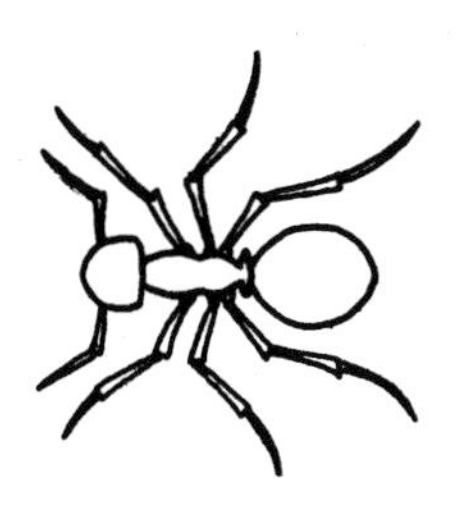

Sea monkeys

- These fascinating creatures are a relative of the shrimp. The eggs are enclosed in crystals so that when they are immersed in water they begin to grow (up to 15 mm). They are available from most large pet stores. All you need is a small, clear container and some water!

Mathematical Development

Use developing mathematical ideas and methods to solve practical problems.

Counting the spots

- Draw, cut out and laminate ladybird shapes.

  Count out six counters and place three on each wing of the ladybird. Ask the children to count the spots and also to say how many spots are on each wing. Write this as a sum: 3 + 3 = 6. Take a spot (counter) from one wing and put it on the other wing. Ask the children how many spots are on the ladybird now. Check which children understand that the total number of spots has not altered. Write the sum to represent the new arrangement of the spots: 4 + 2 = 6. Do the same by moving other spots from one wing to the other. Ask the children how many spots there are in total and what sum would represent the arrangement of the spots.

- Put three spots on one wing and ask the children to match the spots on the other wing.

Counting features

- Look at pictures of insects and spiders and count the number of legs. Ensure that the children are matching pointing with counting.
- Count in twos – eyes, feelers and so on. Demonstrate the counting on a number line.

Spider counting

- Count in tens showing ten fingers to 100. Then show this on a 100 square. If possible, glue a small magnet to the underside of a toy spider and show counting in tens on a magnetic 100 square.

Extension

- Challenge the children to count in tens starting from 2.

Symmetry

- Look at patterns on a butterfly's wings. Explain that they are the same, or 'symmetrical'. Draw some simple butterfly wing outlines and ask the children to make symmetrical patterns with counters. When they understand the concept, ask them to colour symmetrical patterns, using crayons.

Extension

- Give the children one butterfly wing to colour. Give each of them a small mirror and ask what they notice if they stand the mirror on the centre edge of their butterfly wing. Can they draw a second wing to match?

Spirals

- Look at snail shells and observe the spiral patterns. Practise drawing spirals with paints, crayons, charcoal or chalks. Talk about the similarities and differences between spirals and circles.

Music and songs

- Sing 'Five buzzy bees', 'The minibeast parade' and 'Centipede and millipede' from *Tom Thumb's Musical Maths* (see Resources).

Communication, Language and Literacy

Attempt writing for different purposes.

Listening

- Share information books about life cycles, in particular the life cycle of the frog (see Resources).

Writing labels

- Use a square box to record the life cycle of the frog. Turn the box inside out and reglue. Draw pictures of the four stages in the life cycle – eggs (frogspawn), tadpole, tadpole with legs, and frog. On separate pieces of card write labels for each stage and demonstrate how to fix the label with sticky tack to the correct picture. Then ask individual children to come out and fix the labels in the right place. Make several of these boxes with the children's help and hang them as mobiles in or around the role play area. Provide a commentary about the life cycle of the frog and let the children act out each stage.

Music and songs

- Sing 'Tiny caterpillar' from *Bobby Shaftoe, Clap Your Hands* (see Resources).
- Sing 'Creepy crawlies' from *Michael Finnigin, Tap your Chinnigin* (see Resources).

Writing letters

- Talk to the children about the 'Ugly Bug Ball'. Tell them that they need to write letters to their parents telling them about it. Discuss what information will need to go in the letter. Then demonstrate how to write it. Ask the children to help you with some of the writing decisions, such as: Where shall we put this bit of information? What must I remember when writing a name? Constantly reread what you have written and encourage the children to join in.

Extension

- Provide a simple template with basic information – for example, 'Please come to our …' and ask the children to complete the invitation.

Creative Development

Use their imagination in art and design.

Making minibeast headdresses

- Cut strips of card and staple to fit each child. Add features such as eyes, feelers, wings or concertina legs for spiders. Encourage the children to enter the role play area in role as a minibeast. Ask: What dangers lie in wait? How can you protect yourself?

Making a pond scene

- Cut a pond shape out of shiny blue paper. Make reeds from corks impaled on wooden skewers or garden plant support sticks. Add features such as grass or flowers made from tissue paper.

Making frogs

- Fold paper plates in half and paint green or brown. Add large eyes cut from paper, a pipe cleaner tongue and concertina legs.

Making dragonflies and flies

- Cut bodies out of card and add cellophane wings.

Making frogspawn and tadpoles

- Cut irregular shapes of bubble wrap and ask the children to mark dots in some of the bubbles with a permanent marker. With a pencil, draw tadpole shapes on black paper or card and cut out. Stick onto the bubble wrap.

Spiders and webs

- Make spiders from egg-boxes and pipe cleaners. To make a web, dip string into PVA glue and assemble a web shape on the flat side of some bubble wrap. Allow to dry and peel off.

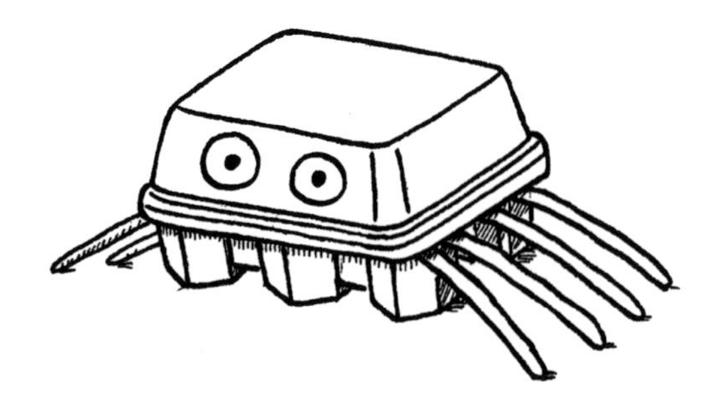

Butterflies

- Either give children a basic butterfly template to draw round or ask them to draw a butterfly with a permanent marker on the flat side of bubble wrap. Then fill the shape with overlapping squares of tissue paper and cellulose paste. Allow to dry, peel off and cut to shape.
- Share the poem 'Butterfly inside (page 35).

Noah's Ark

- Help the children to draw and cut out a large ark shape from corrugated card (neutral shade). Draw, paint or use collage to create pairs of animals. The animals can be displayed suspended from the ceiling, parading in pairs to the ark. Add features to the ark such as lolly stick steps, a dove overhead, and Noah and his family.
- Sing 'Who built the ark?' and 'The ants came marching two by two'.

Ugly bug sweets

- Provide the children with small sweets, such as marshmallows, liquorice laces and dolly-mixtures and some water icing (take care about food colourings!). Let the children create a bug!

Ugly bug ball

- Encourage the children to dress up as bugs (or they can wear headdresses or use sock puppets made in Week 5). They can eat the ugly bug sweets and sing and dance to the Burl Ives song 'The Ugly Bug Ball' (see Resources).

Physical Development

Move with control and coordination.

Spider trap game

- Arrange hoops around the room or playground. Tell the children to scuttle on all fours as insects. They must cross the hoops as they travel. On the command STOP they must stay still where they are. Anyone inside a hoop is caught in the spider's web and is out.

Frogs and ponds game

- Arrange hoops around the room or playground. Tell the children to jump like frogs around the room. On the command INTO THE POND children must jump into a hoop. Remove one hoop each time. Anyone who cannot find a hoop is out of the game and helps you.
- Share the poem 'Jump or jiggle' (page 35).

Review and evaluation

Encourage the children to reflect on the topic. What have they enjoyed learning about? Which part has been most exciting? Which stories and songs do they remember? Which artwork did they most enjoy doing? Which creature did they find most interesting?

Photocopiable

Poems and songs 1

Dinosauristory

Hocus, pocus
Plodding through the swamp,
I'm diplodocus,
Chomp, chomp, chomp!
Grass for breakfast,
I could eat a tree!
Grass for lunch and dinner
And grass for tea.
I'm a diplodocus
Plodding through the swamp,
Hocus-rocus pocus,
Chomp, chomp, chomp!

Judith Nicholls

Hocus, pocus, diplodocus

My name is diplodocus,
I'm the longest of them all.
And what I cannot understand
Is why my brain's so small.
My body's huge
My brain is not.
At thinking fast
I'm not too hot.
In a word,
I'm quite absurd.
Hocus, pocus,
Diplodocus

Tom Stanier

The elephant

The elephant goes like this, like that,
He's terribly big, and he's terribly fat,
He has no fingers, he has no toes,
But goodness gracious me, what a nose.

Anon

One hungry crocodile

One hungry crocodile
Eats two men
Then he eats the others –
How many to make ten?

One hungry crocodile
Eats three men …

(Use raised fingers or line of ten children to indicate number of men eaten)

Anon

Trip to the rainforest

(to the tune of 'Old Macdonald had a farm')

I am going to visit the rainforest
E I E I O
And in the rainforest are some snakes
E I E I O
Big snakes, little snakes, little snakes, big snakes
Fat snakes, thin snakes, thin snakes, fat snakes
I am going to visit the rainforest
E I E I O

(The children do hand actions to indicate the fat/thin snakes. Do the same with monkeys, toucans, sloths.)

Anon

Five little monkeys

Five little monkeys walked along the shore.
One went a-sailing, then there were four.

Four little monkeys climbed up a tree.
One of them tumbled down, then there were three.

Three little monkeys found a pot of glue
One got stuck in it, then there were two.

Two little monkeys found a currant bun
One ran away with it, then there was one.

One little monkey cried all afternoon
So they put him in an aeroplane and sent him to the moon.

Anon

Photocopiable

Alice the camel

(A backwards counting song to the tune of 'Dem bones, dem bones, dem dry bones'.)

(Tell the children to stand together in a circle. They should sing the first four lines and then at the fifth line they should swing their hips and bump together.)

Alice the camel had five humps *(x3)*
So go Alice go.
Boom, boom, boom.

(Continue with four humps, three humps, two humps and one hump. Until...)

Alice the camel had no humps *(x3)*
'Cause Alice is a horse (of course!)

Boa song

I'm being swallowed by a boa constrictor,
boa constrictor, boa constrictor.
I'm being swallowed by a boa constrictor,
Now what do you think of that?
Oh no, he's got my toe.
Oh gee, he's got my knee.
Oh my, he's up to my thigh.
Oh heck, he's up to my neck.
I'm being swallowed by a boa constrictor,
boa constrictor, boa constrictor,
No, no, no. *(Squeaky voice)*

Peggy Drake

Butterfly inside

Caterpillar long *(Stand up.)*
Caterpillar thin *(Arms straight by sides.)*
Caterpillar eat *(Eating action.)*
Caterpillar spin *(Spin round.)*
Caterpillar hush *(Finger to lips.)*
Caterpillar hide *(Hands over face.)*
Caterpillar gone *(Open empty hands.)*
Butterfly inside *(Join thumbs to fly hands.)*

Coral Rumble

Jump or jiggle

Frogs jump
Caterpillars hump

Worms wriggle
Bugs jiggle

Rabbits hop
Horses clop

Snakes slide
Seagulls glide

Mice creep
Deer leap

Puppies bounce
Kittens pounce

Lions stalk –
But –
I walk

Evelyn Beyer

Zoo dream

I dreamed I went
to the zoo one day.
All the animals
came out to play.
There were
Ten whales whistling,
Nine hippos hopping,
Eight monkeys marching,
Seven lions laughing,
Six snakes skipping,
Five donkeys dancing,
Four crocodiles clapping,
Three rhinos roaring,
Two giraffes giggling,
And one seal snoring!

John Foster

Photocopiable

Paper weaving

Photocopiable

Photocopiable

The life cycle of the ladybird

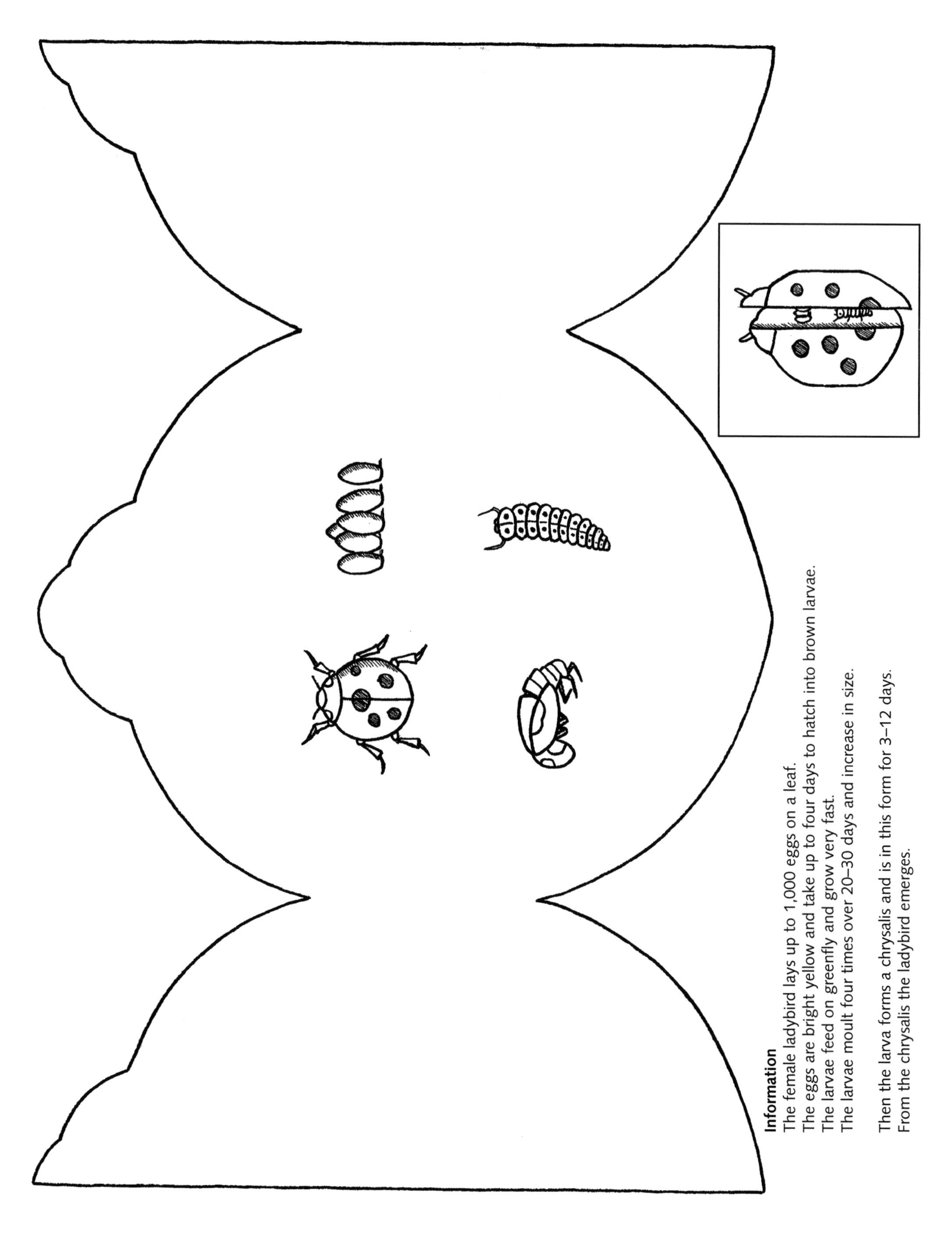

Information

The female ladybird lays up to 1,000 eggs on a leaf.
The eggs are bright yellow and take up to four days to hatch into brown larvae.
The larvae feed on greenfly and grow very fast.
The larvae moult four times over 20–30 days and increase in size.

Then the larva forms a chrysalis and is in this form for 3–12 days.
From the chrysalis the ladybird emerges.

Photocopiable

Observational Assessment Chart

Unit: ____________ **Class:** ____________ **Date:** ____________

Name	Personal, Social and Emotional Development	Communication, Language and Literacy	Knowledge & Understanding of the World	Mathematical Development	Creative Development	Physical Development
	Y B G ELG	Y B G ELG	Y B G ELG	Y B G ELG	Y B G ELG	Y B G ELG
	Y B G ELG	Y B G ELG	Y B G ELG	Y B G ELG	Y B G ELG	Y B G ELG
	Y B G ELG	Y B G ELG	Y B G ELG	Y B G ELG	Y B G ELG	Y B G ELG
	Y B G ELG	Y B G ELG	Y B G ELG	Y B G ELG	Y B G ELG	Y B G ELG
	Y B G ELG	Y B G ELG	Y B G ELG	Y B G ELG	Y B G ELG	Y B G ELG
	Y B G ELG	Y B G ELG	Y B G ELG	Y B G ELG	Y B G ELG	Y B G ELG
	Y B G ELG	Y B G ELG	Y B G ELG	Y B G ELG	Y B G ELG	Y B G ELG
	Y B G ELG	Y B G ELG	Y B G ELG	Y B G ELG	Y B G ELG	Y B G ELG
	Y B G ELG	Y B G ELG	Y B G ELG	Y B G ELG	Y B G ELG	Y B G ELG
	Y B G ELG	Y B G ELG	Y B G ELG	Y B G ELG	Y B G ELG	Y B G ELG

Circle the relevant Stepping Stones (Y = Yellow; B = Blue; G = Green or ELG = Early Learning Goal) and write a positive comment as evidence of achievement.

Photocopiable